Dominick Trant

Observations on the late proceedings in the Parliament of Ireland on the question of a regency for that kingdom

Dominick Trant

Observations on the late proceedings in the Parliament of Ireland on the question of a regency for that kingdom

ISBN/EAN: 9783337174958

Printed in Europe, USA, Canada, Australia, Japan

Cover: Foto ©Andreas Hilbeck / pixelio.de

More available books at **www.hansebooks.com**

OBSERVATIONS

ON THE

LATE *PROCEEDINGS* IN

The PARLIAMENT of IRELAND,

ON THE QUESTION OF A

REGENCY FOR THAT KINGDOM.

[Price a British Shilling.]

OBSERVATIONS

ON THE

LATE *PROCEEDINGS* IN THE

PARLIAMENT of IRELAND;

ON THE

QUESTION

OF A

REGENCY FOR THAT KINGDOM.

BY DOMINICK TRANT, Esq.
ONE OF HIS MAJESTY'S COUNCIL AT LAW IN IRELAND.

QUIS SEPARABIT——?

DUBLIN:
PRINTED BY W. SLEATER, No. 28, DAME-STREET.
MDCCLXXXIX.

OBSERVATIONS

ON THE

LATE *PROCEEDINGS* IN

The Parliament of Ireland, &c.

To form a true judgment of great political transactions, and of the conduct of men concerned in the manangement of publick affairs, it is necessary to look forward into time, and consider how the proceedings of the age in which we live may probably affect the interests of our posterity. —In private life, a prudent father of a family looks beyond his own narrow span of existence, and, in the management of his own present interests, endeavours to promote the prosperity of his descendants: In the great family of the publick, this rule of conduct is still more binding on every good citizen; he poizes, with the utmost circumspection, the good and the evil of every measure of general importance; overleaps the narrow limits of party, of avarice, and of the sordid views of the moment; and, with a liberal and dignified policy, secures the solid and essential interests of generations yet unborn.

By this great rule, applicable to all countries and to all ages, I propose to examine the late proceedings of the two houses of Parliament of this kingdom on the question of REGENCY, and to see how far they tend to counteract, or to promote, the real and permanent interests of the Kingdom of IRELAND.

As countries differ from each other in moral and physical points of view, in situation, laws, religion, original connections, habits, resources, and various other objects of consideration, so must their interests essentially

essentially differ; it is exceedingly difficult to determine, in the abstract, the utmost possible publick good which may be attained in any country; this political problem has been found too difficult for the best Lawgivers, the ablest Statesmen, and the most consummate Writers and Philosophers; the REPUBLIC of PLATO, the UTOPIA of SIR THOMAS MORE, and the OCEANA of HARRINGTON have all been the reveries of great and excellent men, differing from each other in theory, and none of them reducible to practice: Local interests and prejudices, ancient laws and habits, various combinations of internal expediency, numerous relations of external interests and connections, and the great dangers of general innovation, must, when united, place an insurmountable barrier against speculative Politicians.—Men of warm imaginations frequently confound the *possible* with the *probable*, and, having created, by the plastic powers of Fancy, a new people, in a new country, and in the pure state of Nature, they model them at will,

will, and, like the fabled ORPHEUS and AMPHION, build up syftems of focial life and government by the tones of the Lyre, and the powers of Song:—But Judgment and not Imagination fhould lead the practical Politician; He muft fee things as they are, confider what they have been, and weigh well the advantages and difadvantages of any change:—He muft perceive that ftrong expediency fometimes equals neceffity; that the prefent order of things is not always to be violated on the contingency of producing a better, and that the *beft poffible conftitution* is as much a relative term and idea in the Moral, as in the Phyfical, world.

Let us apply this to the political State of Ireland as to its EXECUTIVE GOVERNMENT, as we now find it, and as it has been for many centuries; and to a recent attempt of a Majority of both Houfes of Parliament to alter its frame and conftitution, under the idea of improving its fecurity and independence; and let us confider whether

whether this fuppofed improvement has not been introduced merely to anfwer the purpofes of Party; to delude the warm and honorable affections of the GENTLEMEN of IRELAND often ftrongly inclined to fupport even the appearance of Patriotifm; and whether, in the event, it muft not neceffarily lead to Confequences dangerous to our political Security, fubverfive of our fundamental Laws, and fatal to the eftablifhed Religion and Government of this Country.

The Conftitution of Ireland, as to its Executive Government, as it now is, and as it long hath been, is of a very peculiar nature, formed by a variety of events in our Hiftory, and recognized and declared by our written Laws on principles of Certainty and Wifdom.

From the Conqueft or Acquifition of Ireland by Henry II. and the univerfal Submiffion of the feveral Provincial Kings to that Monarch, as to their Lord Paramount, the Common Law and Conftitution

and

of England became thofe of Ireland, and this Kingdom, under the Name of a Lordfhip, became a Dominion of the Crown of England, infeparably annexed and knit thereto, and dependant thereon; this annexation or dependency, founded on Conqueft, Ceffion, and Acknowledgment, is clearly declared and recognized in many of our Acts of Parliament, fome of which I fhall briefly mention.

The 28th of Hen. VIII. Cap. 2; Entitled, "*An Act of Succeffion of the King and Queen Anne,*" recites that feveral perfons had pretended titles " to the Imperial " Crown of the Realm of England, whereunto this your Land of Ireland is appending and belonging."

28 Hen. VIII. Cap. 3. "*The Act of Abfentees,*"—begins with this recital "Forafmuch as it is notorious and manifeft " that this the King's Land of Ireland, " heretofore being inhabited, and in due " obedience and fubjection unto the King's
" moft

"most noble Progenitors, Kings of Eng-
"land, who in those days, in the right of
"the Crown of England, had great possessi-
"ons, rents and profits within the same
"land, hath principally grown into ruin,"
&c.

And, in another part of the same Act, it is enacted, "That the King, his Heirs,
"and Assigns shall have hold and enjoy,
"as in the right of the Crown of England,
"all Manors, &c." of the Absentees from Ireland therein named.

28 Hen. VIII. Cap. 5, recites in the Preamble "Forasmuch as this Land of
"Ireland is depending and belonging, just-
"ly and rightfully, to the Imperial Crown
"of England" and then enacts "that the
"King our Sovereign Lord, his heirs and
"successors, Kings of the Realm of Eng-
"land, and Lords of this said Land of
"Ireland, shall be accepted, taken and re-
"puted the only supreme head in Earth
"of the whole Church of Ireland, (called
"*Hibernica*

" *Hibernica Ecclesia)* and shall have and
" enjoy, annexed and united to the Imperial
" Crown of England, as well the stile and
" title thereof, as all honors," &c.

28 Hen. VIII. Cap. 6—*the Act of Appeals*, first recites that divers good and wholesome Laws were made in the realm of England for the taking away all Appeals from the Bishop of Rome : and See Apostolick " and forasmuch as this Land " of Ireland is the King's proper Dominion " of England, and united, knit, and belong- " ing to the Imperial Crown of the same " realm, which Crown, of itself, and by itself, " is fully, wholly, entirely and rightfully en- " dowed and garnished with all power, " authority and preeminence &c," and then follows the enacting part, which directs that such appeals shall be brought to the King of England, and Lord of Ireland, his heirs and successors, and further directs that, on such appeal, the Chancellor of England, or Keeper of the great Seal for the time being, shall grant a Commission

or

or delegacy to some discreet and well learned person of this Land of Ireland, or else in the Realm of England, for final determination of all Causes and Griefs in said Appeals, &c.

28 Hen. VIII. Cap. 14. " *An Act for the twentieth part*" enacts " that the King's
" Majesty, his heirs and successors, Kings
" of the realm of England, for more aug-
" mentation and maintenance of the Royal
" Estate of his Imperial Crown, and dig-
" nity of supreme head of the Church of
" England and of Ireland, shall yearly have,
" take, enjoy and receive, united and knit
" to his Imperial Crown for ever, one year-
" ly rent or pension," &c.

N. B. At the time of passing this last mentioned Act, King Henry VIII. was stiled LORD and *not* KING of IRELAND—the Grant was therefore to him, merely as KING OF ENGLAND, and annexed to the Imperial Crown of *that realm*.

28 Hen. 8. cap. 19.—" *The Act of Faculties,*" recites at length the English Act of Faculties, and then, in the 21st Section, proceeds, " Forasmuch as it is mentioned " in the said Act that the effects thereof " should not only extend into the realm " of England and to the commoditie there- " of, and of the subjects of the same, " but also to all other the King's Domini- " ons and his Subjects, and that this the " Land of Ireland is his proper Dominion, " and a member appending and rightfully " belonging to the Imperial Crown of the " said realm of England and united to the " same," &c.

Thus it appears, from the recitals and enacting clauses of these several Statutes, that the Land, Dominion or Lordship of Ireland was, from the first Settlement of the English in this Country, considered as a Member of and belonging to the Imperial Crown of England.—However, as the title of KING founded sweetly in the Ears of the Irish, and the title of LORD, derived from feudal

feudal principles, appeared, to them, comparatively inferior, King Henry VIII. and his Parliament, thought it adviseable to change the title of LORD into that of KING, and recogniz'd and confirmed the original subordination and appendancy of Ireland of the Crown of England by the following Statute—

33 Hen. VIII. cap. 1.—" *An Act that the King of England, his heirs and successors be Kings of Ireland.*"—After reciting that the Kings of England have been Lords of this Land of Ireland, then enacts " that the
" King's Highness, his heirs and successors,
" Kings of England, be always Kings of
" this Land of Ireland, with all manner of
" honours, preeminences, prerogatives,
" dignities and other things, whatsoever
" they be, to the Estate and Majesty of a
" King Imperial appertaining or belong-
" ing, and that his Majesty, his heirs and
" successors, be, from henceforth, named,
" called, accepted, reputed, and taken to
" be Kings of this Land of Ireland, to
" have,

" have, hold and enjoy the said stile, title,
" Majesty and honors of King of Ireland,
" with all manner of preeminence, prero-
" gatives, dignities, and all other the pre-
" mises unto the King's highness, his heirs
" and successors for ever, as united and
" knit to the Imperial Crown of the realm
" of England," &c.

Many other Acts I might adduce, all proving the ancient annexation, subordination and dependency of the Land, Lordship, and Crown of Ireland on the Imperial Crown of England, before any Statute was enacted for that purpose, but I hasten to more modern times, in which this great constitutional point has been proved in actual practice, and confirmed by various Statutes of this Kingdom.

When King James II. in 1688, had abdicated his Crown of England, and, on the 7th of February, 1688-9, the Lords united with the Commons of the Convention Parliament in a vote that the throne was

was vacant, and, by a declaration of the 13th of February, 1688-9; fixed the Crown on the heads of William and Mary, Prince and Princefs of Orange, by *that Vote* and *Declaration* of the Convention Parliament of England King James II. was, *inftantly* and *completely* deprived of all right to the *Crown of Ireland*, though he had not deferted or abdicated the exercife of the functions of *that Crown feparately*, and though the Parliament of Ireland had no fhare in fuch Vote or Declaration, and did not recognize the right of William and Mary till the year 1692, when the firft Parliament after the Revolution was holden in Ireland in the 4th of William and Mary.

It is well known to all, converfant in the flighteft degree with the Hiftory of this Kingdom, that King James's Government was exercifed in full vigour and practice in Ireland, long after the Declaration of Abdication and Vacancy of the Throne, and Settlement of the Crown by the Parliament of England.

England.—There never had been any dereliction, or even suspension, of the Administration of King James *in this Kingdom* until after the battle of the Boyne in July, 1690.—His Lord Lieutenant TYRCONNEL had never been removed from, or disturbed in, his Government, until King James himself arrived in Ireland on the 12th of March 1688-9, from which day, until his shameful flight after the battle of the Boyne, he exercised, *in person*, all the functions of the Crown of Ireland.

Within that period He called a Parliament in Dublin, one of whose first acts was an assertion of the Independency of the Irish Legislature and Courts of Justice, but even they, in their Rage for Reformation and Independence, did not yet think the time ripe for a total separation, nor did they venture, by any solemn act, to sever the Union of the two Crowns, or to disclaim the dependency of that of Ireland on that of England: all their proceedings, however, had a tendency that way, and, if
continued

continued a little longer, muſt have produced the long deſired eternal diſunion of the two Kingdoms.

But the ſucceſs of King William reſtored the old Engliſh Conſtitution of this Country, and the firſt Act of a free and Proteſtant Parliament recognized and confirmed the indiſſoluble union of the EXECUTIVE POWER in both kingdoms, and the dependency of Ireland, in all matters of Imperial Government, on England the Center and main Support of the Empire.

The firſt Parliament of King William and Queen Mary in Ireland paſſed the 4th of W. and M. cap. 1. " *An Act of Recogni-* " *tion of their Majeſties undoubted right to the* " *Crown of Ireland.*"—As this Act clearly recognizes and aſcertains the great point of the ancient union of the two Crowns, and the dependency of that of Ireland on that of England, I ſhall lay it before my readers at full length in the Appendix. Appendix No. 1.

The

The 7th of W. and M. cap. 7. *An Act declaring the Attainders and all other Acts made in the late pretended Parliament to be void,* afcertains this great principle in the ftrongeft manner:—the words of the preamble are, " Forafmuch as fince the happy Acccf-
" fion of his Majefty King William and
" the late Queen Mary of bleffed memory
" to the Imperial Crown of England,
" whereunto this kingdom of Ireland is in-
" feparably annexed, united and belonging,
" no Parliament could or ought to be holden
" within this kingdom, unlefs by their Ma-
" jefties Authority, yet, neverthelefs, divers
" perfons during the late War and Rebel-
" lion in this Kingdom did, on or about
" the feventh day of May, 1689, affemble
" themfelves at or near the City of Dublin,
" without authority derived from their Ma-
" jefties, and in oppofition thereto, and be-
" ing fo affembled did pretend to be, and
" did call themfelves by the name of, a
" Parliament, and, acting in concurrence
" with the late King James, did make and
" pafs feveral pretended Acts or Statutes,
" and

" and did cause the same to be placed and
" recorded amongst the records and pro-
" ceedings of Parliament, all which pre-
" tended Acts were formed and designed in
" manifest opposition to the Sovereignty
" of the Crown of England, and for the
" utter destruction of the Protestants and
" the whole Protestant Interest in this king-
" dom, and are and were null and void to
" all intents and purposes whatsoever."
Then the Act proceeds to direct the cancelling and destruction of the several Acts, Rolls and other Proceedings of the said pretended Parliament, and enacts and declares all such Acts and Proceedings, or pretended Acts and Proceedings, of the said pretended Parliament, to have been from the first making thereof, and now to be, absolutely null and void, to all intents, constructions and purposes whatsoever.

Here we perceive that, by a Declaration of the English Convention Parliament in 1688-9, King James ceased to be, *de Jure et de Facto*, King of Ireland, *tho' he acted as King in Ireland, and with the sanction of an Irish Parliament.*—Such pretended and illegal assumption, or continuance of kingly power in Ireland, after the declaration of vacancy of the English Throne, did not even constitute him *King de facto of Ireland*, in the eye of the succeeding Parliaments from that day to the present period; did not legalize any of his nominations to Office, additions to the Peerage, or other Acts of Royal Authority, or even save his unfortunate adherents in the Irish War of 1689, 1690, and 1691, from the charge and consequences of Rebellion.

Thus we see that the possession of the Crown of England, *quocunque jure*, is considered, by our Laws, as carrying with it the legal title and possession of the Crown of Ireland, and a Case has occurred in our history, where such an event took place, in direct opposition to an Irish Act of Parliament.—I allude to the following instance.

By

By the Irish Act of 28th of Henry VIII. Cap. 2. intitled " *An Act of Succession of the King and Queen Anne,*" the Succession of the Crown of Ireland is, in pursuance of an English Act, settled, in prejudice of the right of the Princess Mary daughter of Henry VIII. and Queen Catherine, on the issue of Henry VIII. and Queen Anne Boleyn, and, *by name*, on the PRINCESS ELIZABETH, yet, on the demise of Edward VI. when Mary was proclaimed, in London, Queen of England, she was, in a few days after, proclaimed Queen in *Ireland*, without any previous consent of the Lords and Commons of this kingdom, in direct opposition to the limitations of the said Irish Act of the 28th H. VIII. Cap. 2. but merely on the ground of her title to the English Crown having been recognised *in England*, and in consequence of the following letter from the Lords of the Council in England to the Lords Justices and Privy Council of Ireland.

E. Rot.
Canc.
Hib.
Anno.
1st
Mary.

Extract — " Ye shall understand our So-
" vereign Lady and Mistress Queen Mary,
" being indeed the very rightful and un-
" doubted heir unto our late Sovereign
" Lord and Master Edward VI. was by us
" yesterday, here in London, proclaimed
" Queen of England, France and Ireland,
" as, by the Proclamation herewith sent,
" ye may perceive, whose Majesty is now
" rightfully and justly possessed of the
" Crown; wherefore we do pray and
" charge you, in her Majesty's name, not
" only to see the said Proclamation pro-
" claimed and set forth to the whole
" realm, but also to cause good Order
" to be taken for the preservation of her
" Majesty's peace, until her Majesty's
" pleasure shall be signified—dated 20th
" July, 1553."

N. B. The inrolment is signed by one of the Lords Justices, and five of the Privy Council of Ireland.

Having thus clearly proved, from our own Laws, that Ireland has, since the acquisition thereof

thereof by the Crown of England, been confidered as *the Dominion of the King of England for the time being, infeparably annexed to and dependant on the Imperial Crown of that realm*, it feems of much weaker and lefs conclufive authority to cite Englifh Statutes in fupport of the fame Doctrine : I fhall therefore omit them.—They are many in number, clear and precife as to the point, and feveral of them have been cited, recognifed and approved by various Acts of the Parliament of Ireland.

The Succeffion to the Crown of England, France and Ireland is fettled by the Englifh ftatute 1^{ft} W. and M. Seff. 2. Cap. 2.—and 12 and 13 W. III. Cap. 2.—the authority of which Acts is fupported and recognifed by the Irifh Acts of 2 Ann. Cap. 5. and 2 Geo. I. Cap. 2.—It is obfervable that thefe Irifh Parliaments of Queen Anne and Geo. I. in paffing thefe Acts did not think themfelves competent to fettle the Succeffion of the Crown of this Realm; they merely recite

the

the Englifh Acts of Succeffion, as neceffarily binding in this Kingdom, and inflict the punifhment of High Treafon on fuch who may be found wicked enough to oppofe them.

It is, by many Acts of the Englifh Parliament, declared to be High Treafon, by writing or otherwife, to deny the power of the King, Lords and Commons to limit, arrange or alter the Succeffion of the Crown of England, and, on fuch limitation by the Legiflature of England, is founded the prefent right of the Houfe of Brunfwick to the Crown of England, France and Ireland, Scotland having acceded thereto by the Act of Union.

Thus we fee that the Succeffion to the Crown of Ireland is now fettled by the Act, not of the Irifh, but of the Englifh, Parliament; let us confider whether this fucceffion, or any fubfequent change therein, can be in any manner affected by the late Acts of the Britifh Parliament repealing the Declaratory

Declaratory Act of the 6 Geo. I. and renouncing all authority to legiflate for Ireland.

No Man will be found fhamelefs enough to affert that, when Ireland afferted her Independency of the Britifh Legiflature, fhe could have thereby propofed to feparate from the Britifh Crown.—It was the declared fenfe of the Irifh Parliament that, on a grant of legiflative Independence to Ireland, no conftitutional queftion could poffibly remain to occafion difpute or jealoufy between both kingdoms—that Ireland was, and muft be for ever, knit to the Crown of Great Britain, and that, fharing the Conftitution of Great Britain, we were determined to fhare her fate, ftanding or falling with the Britifh Nation.

It is therefore clear that, as every modification of the Crown or Executive Power of Great Britain muft neceffarily take effect from the authority of the Britifh Parliament, no Act of that Parliament changing the limitations, or fucceffion of the Britifh Crown,

Crown, fhould be confidered as a Caufe of Jealoufy to Ireland, or a breach of the Act whereby Britain renounced the power to legiflate for Ireland—the infeparable annexation of the Crown of Ireland to that of Great Britain is an original and fundamental Act of Union, prior and paramount to Acts of Parliament, the great cornerftone of fœderal compact, and the unalterable political MAGNA CHARTA of the Conftitution. I believe, therefore, that no Man will be found hardy enough, on reflection, to affert that, as our Law and Conftitution are at this moment fettled, Ireland can have any King but that of Great Britain, by whatfoever title fuch King may hold his Crown, by Act of Parliament or otherwife—the contrary opinion was rafhly hazarded in the warmth of debate, thrown out as the affertion of intemperate party, but unfupported by even the fhadow of argument.—I thought it, however, my duty to clear up this point at length, and by a detail of authorities from our Hiftory and Laws, as, from the infeparable unity of the

Crown,

Crown, I hold it conclusive that the unity of the Executive Power, afsistant to the Crown in both kingdoms, must necessarily follow.

On what great and universal principle is this concurrence of the English and Irish Statutes founded, as to the absolute and necessary indivisibility of the two Crowns?—Certainly on the necessity of providing, in the most effectual manner, for the maintenance of the ancient rights of the English Crown, for the promotion of the solid interests of the subjects of both Countries, and for the support of the English Laws and Constitution granted to, and received by, the People of Ireland; all which salutary purposes can be effectually obtained only by keeping, entire and unimpaired, the Unity of the Supreme Executive and Controuling power of the Empire, in which consists the strength of the whole, and the security of every part, of the British Empire.

Let

Let us first examine, by such lights as History can afford us, the truth of this position that the Executive Power, whether exercised directly by the Crown, or by one or more persons in the name and aid of the Crown, must be always ONE AND THE SAME in both kingdoms, and that the Government of Ireland must necessarily follow the Administration of the Crown of England, as a Satelite follows its primary Planet, as every accessary follows its principal.

I shall produce some of the most memorable instances of English Regencies, and show their influence and controul over the Government of Ireland, almost in every period of our History.

<small>Rymer, 1st vol. passim.

Cox. p. 64, &c.</small>

In the Reign of Henry III. the Earl of Pembroke, by his own authority, assumed the Regency of England during the King's Minority.—The Commissions under the Great Seal of England within that period, of which there are many on Irish business and

and directed to perfons in Ireland, are in the King's name, and generally *Tefte meipfo.*

A. D. 1326.—During the minority of Edward III. the Parliament appointed a Guardian and Council.—Many Commiffions iffued to Ireland under the Great Seal of England as before, *Tefte meipfo,* and fometimes *Tefte Cuftode.* Rymer, Vol. 2

In the firft year of Edward III. while yet a Minor of 14 years of Age, his Guardian and Council iffued letters to Ireland, entitled, " *Literæ mandatoriæ magnatibus Hiberniæ fuper fufceptione regiminis et Jufticiario Hiberniæ conftituto*" they all begin *Rex, &c.*

A. D. 1377.—During the minority of the King, then eleven years old, the Duke of Lancafter and a Council of Regency, appointed by the Parliament of England, governed both Kingdoms.—The Commiffions of this Regency, iffued to Ireland, are, Rymer, Vol. 3.

are, as before, under the Great Seal of England.—One of them is to summon a Parliament in Ireland.

<small>Rymer, Vol. 4.</small>

A. D. 1422.—Henry VI. then an infant nine months old, afcended the throne; during his long minority both Kingdoms were governed by a Regent and Council appointed by the Englifh Parliament: the Commiffions under the Great Seal of England during this minority, many of which are directed to Ireland, are in the King's name, generally *by the Advice and Confent of the Council* and *Tefle meipfo.*

In this Minority, Articles of grievances were fent to the King by the Lord Deputy and the Lords Spiritual and Temporal and Commons of Ireland, praying remedy " *by advice of his right worfhipful and wife Council and Governors;*" and fimilar articles were fent to each of the King's Council or Governors.

A. D.

A. D. 1483. Edward V. then thirteen years old, afcended the throne—the Duke of Glocefter was declared Protector by the Privy Council.—Commiffions iffued to Ireland under the Great Seal of England, as in former Regencies.

A. D. 1546.—Edward VI. became King, then nine years old.—Sixteen Executors, appointed by Henry VIII. under an Englifh Statute, chofe the Earl of Hertford, PRO-TECTOR.—Commiffions to Ireland as in former Regencies. Rymer, Vol. 6.

A Commiffion under the Great Seal of England, in the 1ft. of Edward VI. is di-rected to the Deputy, Chancellor, Vice-Treafurer, &c. of Ireland, returnable into the Irifh Chancery " *faciendi ea omnia quæ in inftructionibus præfentibus annexis exprimuntur.*" *Tefte Rege* 4 *Mar.* 1547. Rymer, 6 Vol.

Who gave thefe inftructions to Ireland? —certainly the Englifh Protector and Council.

4. Ed.

Rolls Office.

4. Ed. VI.—Kings Letter for Sir Thomas Cufack to be Lord Chancellor, and, *inter alia*, for fummoning a Parliament.

Rolls Office.

There are Parliament Rolls in this Regency, tho' there are no Statutes in print—they do not take any notice of the Regency.

Of Regencies fince the Revolution there have been many, particularly in the reigns of W. III. and Geo. I. and II.

By the Englifh Act of $2^{d.}$ W. and M. cap. 6. Queen Mary was appointed Regent in the abfence of King William out of England.—By the $1^{ft.}$ W. and M. Seff. 2. cap. 2. She had no power in the Government, but the whole authority was vefted in King William during his life.—So that Queen Mary's Acts of State and Government, after the $2^{d.}$ of W. and M. cap. 6. were thofe of a Regent under a Statute, and not of a Queen Regnant, and, as Regent, (tho' neither appointed or recognifed by the Irifh Parliament) She iffued Commiffions, &c. under the Great Seal of England to Ireland.

1697. April

1697 April 2.—King William appoints a Council of Regency which governed Ireland without any recognition, and it is obfervable that the Princefs Anne of Denmark, then Heir Apparent, and not merely prefumptive Heir of the Crown, was not included in this Council of Regency—the fame is obfervable in the Regencies of Geo. I. and II.

During thefe Regencies of W. III. and Geo. I. and II. all the Commiffions under the Great Seal of England, directed to this country for the appointment of Chief Governors, Chancellors, &c. are in the King's name, and *tefte'd* by the Regents, and particularly the Commiffions annexed to fuch of the Irifh Bills as paffed during thefe Regencies, of which there are many, authorizing the Chief Governor to give the Royal Affent, are in the King's name, tefted by the Regents, and fubfcribed by " the Guardians and Juftices of the King- " dom."

In 1695 the Lord Deputy in his Speech to the Commons fays, " the Lords Juftices of England have, with great application and difpatch, confidered and tranfmitted all the Bills fent to them."

All the Commiffions, Writs, &c. iffued under the great Seal of the Kingdom of IRELAND for the appointment of Lords Juftices of Ireland, &c. &c. during the period of the feveral Regencies above mentioned, are in the King's name, and tefted by the Chief Governor or Governors of Ireland, and are, in all refpects, in the fame form as at other times, the Regents not being mentioned in them.

Thus it is manifeft, from the whole progrefs of our hiftory, that the perfon or perfons acting in the name and in aid of the Crown of England, in whatfoever manner, or by whatfoever name, appointed, did at all times, thro' the medium of the Great Seal of England, direct and controul the operations of the Government of Ireland,

without

without the appointment, or even the recognition, of the Irish Parliament.—The King's authority, conveyed by the Great Seal of England, gave life and vigour to the general Administration of the whole Empire.—The Chief Governor or Governors here, Officers appointed by the King and his Council of England, and under the Great Seal of England, represented the person and authority of the King, as much in the periods of Regencies, as when the Kings exercised their own personal authority in England; and, as to any acts requiring the Great Seal of Ireland, that was always affixed, by direction of the Governors of this Kingdom, in the name of the King, and without taking notice of the existence of any Regency whatsoever: So that, to all intents and purposes, the existence or non-existence of a Regent was never considered as a point necessarily within the reach or observation of the Irish Parliament, who, equally at all times, saw nothing but the name, authority and seal of the King in all the acts of the executive Government.

Now, in aid of our knowledge derived from hiftory and our records, let us fee whether neceffity, or expediency as ftrong as neceffity, does not require that the fupreme Executive Power, whether ftyled King or Queen, Regent or Protector, Juftices or Council of Regency, muft be one and the fame thro' all parts of the Empire, for all purpofes of general import.—Peace and War, Alliances with Foreign Nations, the maintenance of fimilar Laws in both Kingdoms, and a thoufand other concerns of common import particularly demand, for Great Britain and Ireland, ONE EXECUTIVE, from whofe Adminiftration all the delegated authorities muft proceed—this muft appear indifpenfibly neceffary in every Act of State, and, if poffible, more than in any other proceeding, in the Acts of the Irifh Legiflature, as fettled by our own laws within a very recent period.

By the 21. and 22. Geo. III. cap. 47. No Bill can become an Act of the Irifh Legiflature, unlefs it have previoufly annexed thereto the authoritative Stamp of the Great

Great Seal of Great Britain;—the Irish Parliament confidered this as an unequivocal mark of the approbation of the executive power of Great Britain, and a bond of the union and harmony of both Kingdoms. —The Great Seal of Great Britain being the fole Organ of the publick will, or affent, of the Executive Power of Great Britain, is, of courfe, under the controul and at the difpofal of *that* Executive Power, without whofe confent, therefore, no Bill can pafs in Ireland.

The particular Commiffions, impowering the Chief Governors of this Kingdom to give the Royal Affent to Bills, are always under the Great Seal of Great Britain.— That Symbol alone can convey the Royal Will to the Commiffioner, and he becomes the organ of the Royal Affent to fuch Bills, when *fo impowered*, and not otherwife.

It muft be admitted that, when Ireland affumes the right of naming *her own* EXECUTIVE POWER, fhe fuppofes THAT POWER *neceffarily* invefted with all the rights

rights and ſtrength of effective government, and the Crown's Voice in the Legiſlature; but, it is demonſtrable that, by the Laws of Ireland, ſhe, in naming an EFFECTIVE EXECUTIVE POWER, can only name that of Great Britain.—The power of choice or deliberation being excluded, it ſeems highly ridiculous to aſſert a right of nomination.

But, if the Parliament of Ireland can chuſe and name the Regent of Ireland, ſhe can, and ſometimes poſſibly may, name an Executive Power different from that of England, who muſt, in ſuch caſe, exerciſe the King's Authority without the known Symbol of the Royal Will, and in direct oppoſition to our own Acts of Parliament.—The ſtate of parties may be ſo different in the two kingdoms as that the weaker in Great Britain may prove triumphant in Ireland; this often has been, and will be, the caſe, and, ſurely, it would be highly dangerous to leave the great principle of the Unity of the Empire to the remote chance of two diſcordant parties

parties uniting in the choice of one Object at the Election, particularly when it is confidered that the exaltation of the favourite perfon renders him the decided and effectual Supporter and Protector of that Party to which he owes his elevation.—The greater or leffer degree of fitnefs for that great office will, then, be determined by the interefted judgment of men, pledged to oppofe each other in every thing—thofe judgments will, of courfe, differ ; and that difference will be confidered as a fufficient ground for an oppofite election, and, confequently, for a feparation.

In fuch a cafe, not only a feparation of the Governments of Great Britain and Ireland muft enfue, but a malignant jealoufy, eafily awaken'd into actual hoftility.— The choice of a different Executive power is, in itfelf, a feceffion from the Dominion of the Crown of England, to which this Land of Ireland is, by every Law of this Kingdom, declared to be appendant, annexed and belonging.—It is, in itfelf, a commencement of hoftility not eafily
forgiven

forgiven by a Nation well acquainted with her rights and authority, and well able to aſſert them.

Is there a Man of Engliſh blood in this Country, zealous for the Laws and for the Proteſtant Religion, anxious for the deareſt rights of himſelf and of his poſterity that will riſk the conſequences of ſuch an event——? Our ſituation, our poverty, the nature of our people, the variety and op‑poſition of our different Religions, the claims of our ancient Land-owners or their deſcendants, muſt form an inſuperable bar to any ſtate of abſolute ſeparation from the Crown of England, in which our preſent eſtabliſhed Religion and the intereſts of its profeſſors muſt not be the immediate vic‑tims.—On a ſeparation from England, Ireland, deprived of *her* foſtering Aid and Protection, and confined to her own in‑ternal reſources, muſt neceſſarily expe‑rience the uſual conſequences of a ſtate of Society.—The Intereſts, the Religion and the power of *the few* muſt yield to thoſe of

the

the many.—The prejudices, the paffions, the avarice, the ambition, and what may be called the natural rights of man will be exerted; Eftablifhments, of long ftanding, will be confidered, comparatively, as innovations.—Properties, long fettled, will be attacked as ufurpations; and thofe days of mifery and violence will return, from which no WILLIAM will be found to relieve this devoted Country.

The Experience of the paft Age fhould guide the prefent.—The torch of Hiftory fhould irradiate the policy of nations.—Hiftory is Philofophy teaching by Experience.

What were the great objects of the Parliament of James II. in 1689? What were the means adopted for the attainment of thofe objects? and what muft have been the neceffary confequences of fuch attainment?

The Objects were an entire Separation from the Crown of England—a total and abfolute

abfolute Independence—a King of Ireland *exclufively*—an Annihilation of the Proteftant Religion and of Englifh Influence and Property in Ireland.

The means adopted were,—The formation of a Parliament purely Irifh—Acts of Independency, Attainder, Alteration of the Property of the Church, Revocation of the Act of Settlement, &c. paffed in that Parliament.—Acts of Imperial State of King James, under the Great Seal of Ireland; and, at length, open War againft the Government adopted by the People of England.

If Providence had not interfered and fent the GREAT DELIVERER to the relief of this, then diftracted, Kingdom, what muft have been the Confequences?—Thofe which neceffarily muft arife from natural caufes:—The power of the multitude muft have overborne the refiftance of the few—the great Majority of the People (which a modern Reformer in politics exultingly

exultingly calls the phyſical ſtrength of the Nation) muſt have prevailed·—Property muſt have been reaſſumed—no preſcription of long poſſeſſion would have availed—the weight and authority of offices in every order of the State muſt have followed property, and a Legiſlature, firmly built on that Baſis, would for ever have annihilated the Rights and Liberties, the Laws and the Religion founded by the arms, the wealth, and the protection of England, and cemented by the blood of the Anceſtors of the preſent Legiſlators of Ireland.

I moſt ſincerely believe that many, very many, worthy men, who have ſwelled the majorities in both houſes of Parliament on the late Queſtions, have acted, merely without caution, and not in the idea of furthering a ſyſtem pregnant with ill conſequences: even in the beſt ſuſtained debate, the warmth of party, and the tumult of popular aſſemblies frequently prevent the " ſtill ſmall voice of Reaſon"
from

from being heard :—In the clofet alone do we find time for mature and unbiaffed reflection ;—*there,* the honeft Legiflator will reconfider his actions; will be the fevere critic on himfelf; will diveft himfelf of all prejudice againft Government, and of all attachment to Party; will examine the queftion in every poffible point of view, and, if he fhall difcover his error, will avow his miftake openly and in the face of his Country.—To men of that honourable defcription, and to the landed proteftant Noblemen and Gentlemen of Ireland I particularly addrefs thefe few pages, and now beg leave to call their attention to a brief ftatement of the late proceedings in the Irifh Parliament on the queftion of Regency, and fome Obfervations thereon.—In this Sketch, when I fhall write of men or their meafures, I mean to avoid, all, but public, confiderations ; I have many acquaintances, and I believe fome friends, engaged at each Side of the queftion : Some of thofe whom I moft efteem and love have taken up, on this

this point, ideas of the Conftitution and real interefts of Ireland totally oppofite to mine, and have fupported them, on principle, with a manly and honourable perfeverance and ability; but, I have been early accuftomed to think for myfelf, to examine fuch points as are within my fphere of knowledge, by the beft vouchers and authorities in my power, and, from fuch examination alone, to deduce my own conviction.——" amicus Plato, amicus " Socrates, fed magis amica veritas."

From the day on which the Britifh Lords and Commons affembled after their Prorogation, their attention had been directed to the great and important duty of fupplying the Exercife of the Supreme Executive Power, which had been fufpended by the much lamented indifpofition of his Majefty.—Men of the greateft ability and knowledge, and high in the Councils and Confidence of his Royal Highnefs the Prince of Wales, had, in each Houfe of Parliament, unequivocally afferted his exclufive exclusive right to the Regency as Heir Apparent of full age, and that such right devolved to him necessarily, and as much as the Crown itself would, by Law, descend to him *instanter* on the demise of his Royal Father.

A temporary incapacity was thus compared to a natural demise, and the rule of hereditary and indefeasible right was extended, by the forced construction of men *calling themselves* Whigs and Revolutionists, to a casual and transitory Office of the State, which as occasions may arise, the Constitution of England admits merely as assistant to the Supreme Executive Power: —the People of Great Britain were, by some who *called themselves* Whigs and Revolutionists, to be now deprived of any deliberative voice on a great question of State and Policy, not provided for by any express Statute Law, but which, even in periods of less enlightened freedom, had, in analogous cases, been uniformly referred to the authority and decision of the Parliament,

Parliament, that is, of the People of England.

But the attempt was foon baffled; the uninfluenced Men of the nation, the Country Gentlemen, took the alarm; the friends of the *nominal Whigs* difclaimed, or at leaft foftened, the affertions of thofe unfortunate leaders, and the Prince, whofe benefit they appeared to confult, beft knew his own rights and the privileges of the People in Parliament, from whom alone he meant to deduce his title of Affiftant to his Majefty in the adminiftration of his Government.

A Bill for this purpofe was accordingly, with the Prince's acquiefcence, brought into the Englifh Houfe of Commons, and in its regular train of progrefs, when the Irifh Parliament met on the 5th of February, 1789.

His Excellency the Lord Lieutenant opened the Parliament by a Speech declaring the Indifpofition

indifpofition of his Majefty, on which fubject he laid before them fuch documents as were then in his hands, and expreffed his intention of communicating to them fuch as hereafter might be within his power.

Long before the opening of the Irifh Parliament, it was known what part would be taken on the queftion of Regency, by thofe who have been in the habit of *calling themfelves* the Patriots of Ireland. Many of them had, on former occafions, decidedly ranged themfelves under the Standard of that great Englifh Party which had long been under eclipfe, but which was foon expected to fhine with redoubled light and influence; the Policy of the Englifh Oppofition had long been directed to the maintenance of a fubordinate Party in Ireland, pledged to rife or fall with their Englifh friends and creators; fome of the Chiefs of this Irifh Confederacy had, about this time, taken their annual flight to England to receive new lights and infpiration at the fhrine of POLITICAL VIRTUE, and, with them

them, migrated fome callow birds who tried unfledged wings under the guidance of their more experienced leaders.

Behold them now returned, having fate on the facred Tripod, and full of the God!—On the benches of both Houfes they were reinforced by many auxiliaries, who, deep in all the maxims of wordly prudence, confidered the ftrong fide as always the beft, and who, with the fondeft eagernefs, look'd forward to new times, as productive of new emoluments:—Having exhaufted the favours of a liberal and indulgent Government, they fought for further Supplies in the gratitude of a new and fplendid Adminiftration; by plucking off the right of Majefty from the Parent Tree, they expected to fee a new branch haftily produced, which, to them, fhould fhine with equal, or fuperior fplendor and advantage:

" ―――― Primo avulfo non deficit alter
" Aureus, et fimili frondefcit virga metallo :"

The popular director in the Houfe of Commons faw, with joy and aftonifhment, men of various defcriptions, of different countenances,

nances and complexions, ranged in Battalia around him;—like Mithridates, he fpoke to each in his own language, flattered their hopes, foothed their prejudices, received their repentance, granted them abfolution for all their political fins, and prevailed on his ancient forces to receive their new allies with every mark of joy and gratulation.

A prudent and experienced General claffes his forces according to their different powers, arms, nations, and properties, and gives them diftinctive names accordingly—this latter body was known by the name of RATS, from a familiar allufion to the known and prudent inftinct of thofe animals, in quitting a falling houfe or a finking fhip, and much was expected from the defperate valour of thofe deferters, who, on the defeat of their army, according to the rules of war, could never expect quarters.

Difappointment added many to the affociated army.—The public œconomy of the oppofite opposite General, was on too contracted a scale for their enlarged power of expenditure.—He discouraged marauding and foraging, and endeavoured to revive the long obsolete ideas of Roman disinterestedness and Spartan discipline :—his Commissaries were obliged to account and make true musters; his purveyors of ammunition and stores were kept to their duty or severely punished.—The People, who were thus protected from pillage and peculation, blessed him, but his army crumbled away at every moment, such was the contagious power of Mutiny and Desertion.

At some distance from this motley band were seen some whose Love of their Country, whose Ability and Integrity, had never been doubted, and frequently been proved on the most trying occasions:—in some occasional movements they were now seen under the Standard of Opposition, but they demonstrated the integrity of their principles by scorning a blind adherence to the dictates of Party, and by refusing to be

E the

the dupes and accomplices of an ill-timed and misguided resentment.

An Address to the Prince of Wales passed the House of Commons, praying him to assume the Royal Authority in Ireland without any restriction whatsoever—this Address was conceived in extreme haste, drawn up in much confusion, and passed with little consideration; it was opposed by Law and Reason, but supported by the magical power of numbers; it purported to convey, on the instant of an answer in the affirmative, and without any subsequent connected Law, the whole royal prerogative to the Prince of Wales; to divest the King of the exercise of his Royal power, on the mere faith of copies of reports of Physicians not under the controul or examination of our Parliament, and with no consideration of the proceedings of the British Parliament, unless when abused by some zealous members, who contrasted them with the enlightened, the manly, and the constitutional conduct of that of Ireland.

The

The Addrefs, thus hurried thro' the Houfe of Commons, was ufhered into the Houfe of Lords.——There, many of the wifeft and oldeft of thofe hereditary Counfellors of the Crown faw its tendency, and oppofed it accordingly.—Others of the moft upright and able, adopted it as a proof of the refpect of Ireland to the intended Regent; as, in itfelf, conveying no Authority or Regal Power but merely preparatory to a Law for that purpofe; and fuch were the public declarations in full Parliament, on this fubject, of * two of the moft able, refpectable, and experienced Lords, who ever fat in any Houfe of Parliament.

Thus, fupported by a combination of various motives; and on different conftructions, grounds and principles, the ADDRESS was voted by the Houfe of Lords, with fome Amendments expreffive of a decent condoleance on the dreadful Malady of the Sovereign, which the framers of the Addrefs in the Houfe of Commons had, in their

---
* The Archbifhop of Cafhel, and Lord Vifcount Pery.

their great hafte, either cafually omitted, or thought entirely unneceffary.

The ADDRESS, finally adopted by both Houfes, was prefented to the Lord Lieutenant, to be, by him, tranfmitted to the Prince of Wales.

The Lord Lieutenant, relying on his official duty, on the terms and import of his Oath of Office, and not thinking himfelf warranted to tranfmit fuch an Addrefs to the Prince of Wales 'till he fhould, by Law, be appointed Regent, declined to tranfmit the Addrefs.

It is clear that the Lord Lieutenant, who is *here* as an Officer or Deputy of the Crown of Great Britain, and appointed by the King, in his Britifh Council, under the Great Seal of Great Britain, ftands merely intermediate between the King, or Executive power of the Crown, and the Parliament or People of Ireland:—He is the Channel of communication from the Crown

to

to the Parliament, and *vife verfâ*, having himfelf no official communication or correfpondence with any perfon or power in Great Britain, but with the King, thro' the medium of his Minifters in their feveral departments—; thus circumftanced, the Lord Lieutenant, as Lord Lieutenant, cannot convey any meffage, addrefs or other intimation of the will of the Parliament of Ireland, to any Subject whatfoever, nor, of courfe, to the Prince of Wales the firft of the Kings Subjects :—If he fhould ever, in the hour of imprudence and precipitation, convey any Addrefs to a fubject, fimilar to that which he was thus defired to tranfmit, he would probably be thought, by his Peers of Great Britain, fubject to capital punifhment, as a betrayer of the RIGHTS of his SOVEREIGN, and of the ANCIENT FŒDERAL CONSTITUTION OF THE BRITISH EMPIRE.

The Spirit of Party, however, was inflamed to double violence, and the Lord Lieutenant's refufal to tranfmit the . Addrefs,

Addrefs, as expreffed in his Anfwer, was confidered as a Breach of the Privileges of both Houfes of Parliament, and a Cenfure of their Proceedings.—In vain it was urged in both Houfes that, without a knowledge of the Lord Lieutenant's Patent, and of his Oath of Office, Parliament could not judge how far he might have been really bound by his official Duty and his Confcience, to return fuch an Anfwer; fruitlefs attempts were made to induce both Houfes to have thofe documents laid before them, as the only folid grounds of unbiaffed and honourable Judgment: Votes of Cenfure paffed with the ufual precipitancy.

In thefe ill-digefted and hafty meafures, it is obfervable, that many of the moft dignified fupporters of the Addrefs in both Houfes did not concur.——They clearly faw that thofe with whom they had hitherto acted on the queftion of Regency, were now proceeding much too far, and refufed to lend the fanction of their fupport support to party-violence, or to private resentment.

There are cases in which the Pupil overleaps the bounds prescribed to him by his master, and the labourer transgresses the orders of his employer. It is clear that the British Opposition, which had, as far and as long as prudence would permit, asserted the exclusive right of the Prince of Wales to the Regency, must have intended that this doctrine should be adopted and reduced to practice in Ireland, and must have issued out *orders* for that purpose; but those who were to execute those orders, thought it dangerous to propose such a doctrine to the people of Ireland, whose principles were those of the REVOLUTION, or judged it right to sink, in silence, the rights of the Heir Apparent, and give the preference to the right of election or nomination of the Parliament of Ireland, thereby more fully to effect that Separation of the two kingdoms which, under the title of total Independency, they had so long and so earnestly promoted; a Resolution accordingly

accordingly paffed both Houfes " That in " addreffing his Royal Highnefs the Prince " of Wales to take upon himfelf the go- " vernment of this Country on the behalf " and in the name of his Majefty, during " his Majefty's prefent indifpofition and no " longer, the Lords and Commons of Ire- " land have exercifed an undoubted right, " and difcharged an indifpenfible duty, to " which, in the prefent emergency, they " alone were competent," by which Refo- lution, the rights of the Prince of Wales, and of the Parliament of Great Britain, are *equally* abjured.

The Lord Lieutenant having thus declin- ed to tranfmit the Addrefs to the Prince of Wales, the conveyance was intrufted to fome Members of both Houfes: Some, who fhuddered at the ill confequences which might arife, if this Addrefs fhould reach the Prince of Wales, before he fhould be appointed Regent of Great Britain, requeft- ed a little delay:—urged the general ex- pectations which were then gaining ground.

of

of the King's approaching recovery—insisted on the inutility of precipitation in this bufineſs, as the Prince would certainly be appointed Regent in Great Britain, if the King's indifpofition ſhould ſtill continue, and that the decifion of the queſtion of *Iriſh Right* would, on the prefent occafion, be therefore totally unneceſſary——all this was whiſtled to the winds—the great Leader of the Majority in the Houfe of Commons contended that *the Principle* ſhould not be given up; that the ſlighteſt delay would be confidered as a relinquiſhment of it *in theory*, and that there could not, be, in this cafe, any poſſible riſk *in practice*, as the Prince would *certainly* be appointed Regent of Great Britain before the arrival of the Iriſh Commiſſioners, Delegates, or Meſſengers, in London.

Tho' I have, in truth, the higheſt Opinion of the extraordinary talents and merit of the Gentleman who returned this anſwer, yet I do not worſhip him with all the blind zeal of idolatry, nor do I conceive him,

like

like the Adam of the Schoolmen, intuitively gifted with *all poffible knowledge*. On *this Occafion* he was no Prophet—the Commiffioners arrived in London, where no Regent was yet appointed—the Prince received the addrefs; but the imprudence and danger of his deciding this queftion in favour of the newly affumed right of the Irifh Parliament were obvious;—delay was therefore interpofed, and the happy event of the complete recovery of his Majefty enabled the Prince to get out of his embarrafsment, by declining the offer of Ireland with the utmoft Civility, after having received the Commiffioners at Carleton-Houfe, with all the Condefcenfion imaginable.

Let us now confider whofe Interefts, Rights and Privileges (next to thofe of his Majefty) are moft immediately and directly injured by the late proceedings in the Irifh Parliament, fmoothing the ground for a future feparation of the Executive Powers of the two kingdoms.

In the firſt inſtance, clearly, thoſe of the Prince of Wales, who, in the fulneſs of time, we all moſt ſincerely hope and truſt, will be the Sovereign Ruler of theſe kingdoms.

Can it be a pleaſing conſideration to his Royal Highneſs, that a foundation is now laid for the future poſſible diſunion of the two Governments, when, in the caſe of minority, abſence, or other temporary incapacity of the reigning King, there may be a neceſſity for eſtabliſhing a Regency by Act of Parliament or otherwiſe? Can his Royal Highneſs ſee, without abhorrence, the conduct of men, calling themſelves his friends, who wiſh to build up for him a ſupport in Ireland, diſtinct from, and oppoſite to, that of his future Parliament and People of Great Britain; of men who ſow the ſeeds of mutual jealouſy, and enmity between both kingdoms by unneceſſarily forcing on the diſcuſſion of a queſtion, the deciſion of which, points to a poſſible, if not a probable, ſeparation? Will his Royal Highneſs, even for a moment, be
prevailed

prevailed upon to turn his eyes from the great Precedent of the REVOLUTION, which feated his moſt illuſtrious family on the throne of both kingdoms, and which was binding *in Ireland* merely becauſe it had taken place and been confirmed *in England*, and will he not conſider the dignities, prerogatives and intereſts of his future Royal Crown, and that of his Succeſſors, materially impaired and injured by any Act which directly and neceſſarily weakens the connection of the two Kingdoms now mer ly ſupported by that ſingle thread, THE UNITY OF THE EXECUTIVE POWER? His Royal Highneſs's moſt liberal an unſuſpecting diſpoſition, may hitherto have prevented his ſeeing this tranſaction in its proper light;—his open and grateful heart prompts him to receive, with acknowledgement, the proffered ſervices of thoſe who aſſume an appearance of decided and forward zeal for, what they call, his intereſts; and his moſt benevolent and honourable feelings become two ſtrong for his moſt excellent and diſcerning Judgment—his

very

very Virtues thus unfortunately tend to promote and lengthen the delusion.

But, as TIME, in his rapid flight, bears TRUTH along with him, fhe will prefent her Mirror to the eyes of the PRINCE, in which he will behold, with aftonifhment and regret, the real nature, object and effect of all thefe late proceedings of his pretended friends and adherents; and he will then, and, I truft, not too late, learn to value, efteem and protect thofe who are now pointed out to him as his oppofers and enemies.

The next clafs of fufferers, in the future threatened calamity of a feparation of the Executive Power of the two kingdoms, is that of the prefent landed Intereft of Ireland, whofe tenures, offices, dignities and fuperior advantages under the prefent Conftitution of Ireland, muft fink into the general mafs, or be holden at the difcretion of an adverfe and interefted Majority of the People.

Need

Need I again mention that the Rulers and Paſtors of the preſent eſtabliſhed Church of Ireland, and all who profeſs or call themſelves Proteſtants among us, under whatſoever denomination, will neceſſarily become, in every conſideration of temporal intereſt and religious freedom, materially injured by any diſunion of the *Executive Power*, and by any Act which can render Great Britain unconnected with, or indifferent to, the civil and religious eſtabliſhments of Ireland.

In ſhort, all men now in Office, poſſeſſed of dignities in Church or State, poſſeſſed of Eſtates under Engliſh Titles, whether of ancient or modern date, from the original ſettlement of the Engliſh to the preſent moment, all the hereditary Counſellors of the Crown, all who are, or, under the preſent Laws, expect to be Members of the Legiſlature, all who have Votes or any other Franchiſes above the maſs of the People, all who have any particular weight or influence in the Legiſlature of this kingdom

kingdom as at prefent fettled, and all who, on liberal and general principles, wifh to promote the folid and real interefts of the whole Empire, muft fuffer by the late innovation, muft abjure its principles, and muft, on mature reflection, chearfully promote, recommend, and concur in any effectual remedy which may be propofed, for the prevention of the threatened evil, the SEPARATION of the NOW UNITED EXECUTIVE POWER.

Parliament which in the hour of heat, of party, and of intereft, admitted that Propofition which awakes the apprehenfions of every thinking man in both kingdoms, can alone apply the remedy:—The ruft of the Spear of Achilles could alone cure the wound it had inflicted—an Appeal was fuccefsfully made from PHILIP to himfelf, from PHILIP heated and intemperate, to PHILIP cool and difpaffionate;—the Monarch gained immortal Glory by redreffing the injuftice which he had committed.

In

It cannot be controverted, that Laws are made to procure certainty and decifion in all cafes which can be the natural objects of Legiflation, and within the power of human prudence to forefee: On that principle, Laws are framed for directing the Succeffion of the Crown, tho', in the courfe of events, a cafe may occur beyond the reach of thofe Laws, and which, by it's infinite magnitude or danger, may render it neceffary to recur to firft principles, and, in preference to all written or fettled Ordinances, to appeal to the fupreme and original power of the people.—Tho' fuch fingular cafes may arife and juftify a deviation from the known and ordinary fyftem, as in the cafe of the GLORIOUS REVOLUTION, yet, it muft be admitted, that Laws are to be enacted for the maintenance of the general order and conftitution, and without fuppofing the probable exiftence of fuch future exception, which muft be a breach of the Law, juftified only by the ftrongeft neceffity.

Thus

Thus, tho' the hereditary Succeſſion hath been altered and diverted from its original courſe by the Revolution, yet the Law of hereditary deſcent of the Crown, is ſtill the acknowledged and general Law; and tho' the Power of the People ſtill remains undiminiſhed and Supreme, yet the Law will not ſuppoſe the probability of any future neceſſity of a ſuſpenſion of its own operation.

On this principle, tho' I hold it poſſible, that a Caſe might occur, in which neceſſity may juſtify the People of Ireland, in ſeparating from the Crown of England, yet the Law does not ſuppoſe ſuch a Caſe, and, therefore, the Law of Union of the two Crowns is poſitive and unconditional—the poſſible contingent Abuſe of a Law, ſo ſtrong as to force a recurrence to a diſſolution of Compact, and a breach of the Conſtitution, merely to preſerve political exiſtence, does not, by any means, weaken the Authority of the Law, as the univerſal rule

rule founded on the ftrongeft principles of Policy and Juftice.

By this rule of reafoning let us examine the arguments of fome members of both Houfes of Parliament in juftification of their precipitancy in forcing the nomination of a Regent for Ireland, before any Regency had been fettled in Great Britain.

They argued that, as a Cafe might occur, in which, the nomination of a Britifh regent may be fo grofsly mifdirected by the violence of party, the corruption of influence, or the ufurpation of violence, as that the choice fhould be made of a perfon or perfons grofsly and apparently unfit for the truft, decidedly inimical to the rights and liberties of the people, and peculiarly hoftile to the commerce, rights, and privileges of Ireland; therefore, in *this Cafe*, where no fuch danger was threatened, and where the object of our own predilection was known to be the intended Regent

of

of Great Britain, we fhould decidedly deviate from the ufual and fettled forms and principles of the Conftitution :—They argued that we were bound to acknowledge the King of Great Britain, merely becaufe we had fo fettered ourfelves by our own written Laws, and that, as the cafe of Regency was not included in the exprefs provifion of thofe Laws, however included virtually by every principle of analogy, of policy, and of common fenfe, we fhould take the advantage of this omiffion, and, without any neceffity in this particular inftance, boldly form a precedent of a poffible feparation.—They did not wifh that we fhould have time to confider that it is highly dangerous to break through the fettled habits and the unwritten practice of the Conftitution without the moft urgent neceffity; that it is impolitic and dangerous to introduce, *familiarly, and as of courfe*, thofe violent remedies which fhould be referved merely as the laft refources of agonizing nature; and that Revolutions, frequently and unneceffarily introduced,

F 2　　　　　　would

would soon destroy our respect for the Laws, and shake our frame of Government to its very foundation.

We have, in this late instance, seen a precedent established, of an easy separation of the executive powers of Great Britain and Ireland, without flow and regular deliberation, without the plea of necessity, and against the decided sense of all the great lawyers in both Houses of Parliament.—We have heard this extraordinary deviation from settled rule justified, merely on the plea of having *no written* Law, *expressly and in words*, ascertaining the Constitution of the united Empire in the *Case of Regency*; and no man has been found hardy enough to assert that, if a written law were now existing on that point, there is, in the present instance, any necessity of recurring to first principles or of deviating from the regulations of the Law.

He therefore will be the real friend of his Country who proposes, and who procures the

the paffing of fuch a Law, by which the Regency of the two Kingdoms may be fettled on principles of general certainty and found policy, as the Union of the two Crowns is now afcertained:—He will prevent many future ftruggles for power, many party animofities, many dangerous civil diffentions which may hereafter arife from the inequality of the great contending parties in both Kingdoms:—By fuch a Law the general expediency, and even the political neceffity, of an uniformity of Government in both Countries will be confirmed and afcertained; by fuch a Law, no great and urgent cafe of neceffity, threatening the diffolution of civil and religious rights and liberties, can be fuperfeded, and yet, the refpect due to fuch a law will prevent its infringement on any, but the moft abfolutely important, occafions:—By fuch a Law, *paffed in our own Parliament*, the dignity of our own Legiflature will be fupported even according to the warmeft wifhes of the moft independent fon of Ireland; by fuch a Law alone can we prevent the various ill
confequences

confequences which may fpeedily arife from the hafty and unneceffary feparation of the two executive powers; confequences fatally affecting our Properties, our Laws, and our Religion; by fuch a Law alone can we become a firm and component part of a great Empire, connected by the great bond of ONE KING, ONE FAITH, AND ONE LAW; and by fuch a Law alone can we fulfil our folemn affurances, made on the reftoration of our Parliamentary independence, that We will fhare the fate of Great Britain, having one common and indiffoluble intereft with her's, and ftanding or falling with the Britifh nation.

When I confider that, in the late proceedings, Majorities were raifed in both Houfes of Parliament of perfons acting together under various motives, fome actuated by felf-intereft, many by private refentment for fuppofed infults or unmerited difappointments, others by the eager hope of recommending themfelves to the notice

and

and protection of the expected Adminiftration, and fome from the apprehenfion of forfeiting their prefent fituations by a fruitlefs defence of their Royal Mafter, I cannot think that fo heterogeneous a body can long remain united: On the mixture of different fubftances, of various weights and properties, their union only continues as long as they are kept in violent agitation—when that ceafes, their repelling or their attractive powers, their greater or leffer gravity, in fhort their various and oppofite properties will caufe them to take their own places according to the fixed laws of matter.—Time and reflection, and the confideration of publick good and private intereft, will produce the fame effects in our prefent fermenting mixture; and the lead and the feather, the oil and the vinegar, the gold and the drofs, will all foon fubfide and form their regular ftrata in political tranquility.

The attempt will be found vain to unite men of various and oppofite principles in one great chain of confederacy; affociations, folemn solemn leagues and covenants, writings and seals may be suggested by those who clearly see that there is no cementing principle of public Virtue to strengthen the building, but such miserable expedients will be found of no avail; the general voice of the nation will be raised against those dark and secret proceedings usual only among those who conspire the destruction of States and the dissolution of Society. The enlightened men without doors, men who constitute the bulk of the Electors of the Nation, will see the danger of intrusting the care of their rights and liberties, of their commerce and properties, to representatives who assemble in solemn and mysterious silence, and pledge themselves to some mode of obstructing the regular and necessary business of Government, in the due and ordinary revolution of which the interest of every citizen is essentially concerned.—The mysteries of the Eleusinian CERES were deceits on the credulity of ancient Greece, but the Philosophers saw, and despised, the imposition.—The silence of those who descended into

the

the Cave of TROPHONIUS could not preferve the Deity and the Priefts from detection and contempt.

PUBLIC VIRTUE is of an open and dignified countenance, placed in general view, on the fummit of the hill, and beaming, in full Majefty, from the front of her temple:—PARTY fcoops her cavern in the neighbouring clift, overfhadowed with yew, and impervious to the Sun:—her Votaries approach her Shrine in the dead hour of night; they murmur their vows indiftinctly; they mine in fecret, and unite, in vain, to fap the eternal foundations of the facred FANE of VIRTUE.

The ardent wifhes of every true friend of this country muft be directed to the eftablifhment of a folid and permanent union of her Executive Power with that of Great Britain; that alone can fecure their harmony and unanimity, without which the nerves and finews of the Empire muft be weakened and contracted; that alone can

prevent

prevent the pernicious effects of thofe daily ftruggles for power which muft endanger the connection of the two kingdoms, if not placed on an unqueftionably legal foundation:—that alone can fave from deftruction the liberties, the interefts and the eftablifhed religion of Ireland, which muft neceffarily be annihilated when unconnected with Great Britain;—and this good work can be folidly effected by our own Parliament, without yielding even the appearance of fuperior authority to any other body or power whatfoever.

I have no doubt that, in a period not very diftant, the moft able, upright and difpaffionate among the Legiflators of Ireland will fee the neceffity of placing this great point of national importance beyond the reach of tranfitory interefts, of cafual circumftances, and of the moft uncertain fluctuations of party:—a cloud now hangs on the brow of every thinking man in Ireland, which they alone can remove; they alone can diffipate thofe doubts which, from

from some late transactions, the Electors of this Kingdom begin to entertain of the wisdom, the coolness, the moderation, and the temperate and well regulated patriotism of their Parliaments; they alone can restore dignity to the State, effect to the Government, security to the Religion, and stability to the Laws, the Interests, and the Constitution of Ireland.

APPENDIX.

APPENDIX.

The Fourth Year of WILLIAM and MARY.

CHAP. I.

An Act of recognition, of their Majesties undoubted Right to the Crown of Ireland

FORASMUCH as this kingdom of Ireland is annexed and united to the Imperial Crown of England, and by the laws and statutes of this kingdom is declared to be justly and rightfully depending upon, and belonging, and for ever united to the same; and the Kings and Queens of England are by undoubted right Kings and Queens of this realm, and ought to enjoy the stile, title, majesty, power, preeminence, jurisdiction, prerogative and authority of Kings and Queens of the same: and whereas our sovereign liege lord and lady, King William and Queen Mary, since their happy accession to the crown of England, with great expence of blood and treasure, and the extreme hazard of his Majesty's royal person, have delivered this their kingdom from the miseries and calamities of an intestine war, and most horrid rebellion, raised up amongst us by the Irish papists, and instigated, abetted and supported by the power of the French King; thereby securing us against the danger of popery and arbitrary power, with which we were threatened in a most eminent manner, and have most happily reduced this their kingdom to a state of peace and order, and restored to us our laws and liberties, and the free and impartial administration of justice: we the lords spiritual and temporal and commons in this present Parliament assembled, in the name of all the people of this kingdom, do, from the bottom of our hearts, with all possible thankfulness acknowledge the goodness of Almighty God, in raising up their Majesty's to deliver us and to reign over us, of whose goodness, wisdom and courage, we have already found such happy and blessed effects.

II. And to the intent and purpose, that we may publickly and unanimously own and assert our faith and true allegiance to their Majesties, and that the same may remain as a memorial to all posterity amongst the records of Parliament in this kingdom: we the lords spiritual and temporal and commons in Parliament assembled, as we are in duty bound

bound, do recognize and acknowledge, that the kingdom of Ireland, and all titles, ftiles, royalties, jurifdictions, rights, privileges, prerogatives, and preeminences-royal thereunto belonging, are moft rightfully and lawfully vefted in their Majefties King William and Queen Mary, and that their moft excellent Majefties were, are, and of right ought to be King and Queen of England, Ireland, Scotland, and France, and the dominions and territories thereunto belonging; in and to whofe princely perfons the royal ftate, crown, and dignity of the faid realms, with all honours, ftiles, titles, regalities, prerogatives, powers, jurifdictions, and authorities to the fame belonging and appertaining, are more fully, rightfully and intirely invefted and incorporated, united and annexed.

III. And we do befeech their moft excellent Majefties, to accept of this our humble recognition and fubmiffion, as the firft fruits in this prefent Parliament of our faith and duty to their Majefties; and do pray that the fame may be publifhed, declared, and enacted in this high court of Parliament; and the fame are by their faid Majefties, by and with the advice and confent of the lords fpiritual and temporal and commons in Parliament affembled, and by the authority of the fame, declared, enacted, and eftablifhed accordingly.

The following is the Addrefs to the Prince of Wales, as it firft paffed the Commons, February 12th 1789.

To his Royal Highness
GEORGE, PRINCE of WALES.

The humble ADDRESS of

The KNIGHTS, CITIZENS, and BURGESSES,

In Parliament Affembled,

May it please your Royal Highness,

WE, his Majefty's moft dutiful and loyal fubjects, the Commons of Ireland in Parliament affembled, beg leave humbly to requeft that your Royal Highnefs will be pleafed to take upon you the government of this realm during the continuation of his Majefty's prefent indifpofition, and no longer, and under the ftile and title of Prince Regent of Ireland, in the name and on behalf of his Majefty, to exercife and adminifter, according to the laws and conftitution of this kingdom, all regal powers, jurifdiction and prerogatives to the crown and government thereof belonging.

The

[81]

The following is the Addreſs which paſſed both Houſes of Parliament, to his Royal Highneſs, the Prince of Wales. February 17th 1789.

TO HIS ROYAL HIGHNESS,

GEORGE, PRINCE of WALES.

THE HUMBLE ADDRESS OF THE LORDS SPIRITUAL and TEMPORAL, and KNIGHTS, CITIZENS, and BURGESSES, in Parliament Aſſembled,

MAY IT PLEASE YOUR ROYAL HIGHNESS,

WE, his Majeſty's moſt dutiful and loyal ſubjects, the Lords Spiritual and Temporal and the Commons of Ireland, in Parliament aſſembled, beg leave to approach your Royal Highneſs with hearts full of the moſt loyal and affectionate attachment to the perſon and government of your royal father; to expreſs the deepeſt and moſt grateful ſenſe of the numerous bleſſings which we have enjoyed under that illuſtrious houſe, whoſe acceſſion to the throne of theſe realms has eſtabliſhed civil and conſtitutional liberty

upon

upon a bafis which, we truft, will never be fhaken; and at the fame time, to condole with your Royal Highnefs upon the grievous malady with which it has pleafed heaven to afflict the beft of fovereigns.

We have however the confolation of reflecting, that this fevere calamity hath not been vifited upon us until the virtues of your Royal Highnefs have been fo matured as to enable your Royal Highnefs to difcharge the duties of an important truft, for the performance whereof the eyes of all his Majefty's fubjects of both kingdoms are directed to your Royal Highnefs.

We therefore beg leave humbly to requeft that your Royal Highnefs will be pleafed to take upon you the government of this realm during the continuation of his Majefty's prefent indifpofition, and no longer, and under the ftile and title of Prince Regent of Ireland, in the name and on behalf of his Majefty, to exercife and adminifter, according to the laws and conftitution of this kingdom, all regal powers, jurifdiction and prerogatives to the crown and government thereof belonging.

Lord

Lord Lieutenant's Answer, on being desired to transmit the Address to the Prince of Wales. February 19th 1789.

UNDER the impressions which I feel of my official duty, and of the oath which I have taken as Chief Governor of Ireland, I am obliged to decline transmitting this address into Great Britain.

" For I cannot consider myself warranted to lay before the Prince of Wales an address, purporting to invest his Royal Highness with powers to take upon him the government of this realm before he shall be enabled by law so to do.

Vote or Resolution of Censure, of the Lord Lieutenant's Answer, by the House of Commons. February 20th 1789.

Resolved, that his Excellency the Lord Lieutenant's answer to both Houses of Parliament, requesting him to transmit their Address to his Royal Highness the Prince of Wales, is ill advised, contains an unwarranted and unconstitutional censure on the proceedings of both Houses of Parliament, and attempts to question the undoubted rights and privileges of the Lords Spiritual and Temporal, and the Commons of Ireland.

Vote or Resolution of Censure, of the Lord Lieutenant's Answer by the House of Lords. February 23ᵈ 1789.

Resolved, that the Answer of his Excellency the Marquis of Buckingham the Lord Lieutenant of Ireland, refusing to transmit to Great Britain, the Address of both Houses of Parliament, to his Royal Highness the Prince of Wales, was disrespectful to his Royal Highness, and conveys an unwarrantable Censure on both Houses of Parliament.

www.ingramcontent.com/pod-product-compliance
Lightning Source LLC
Chambersburg PA
CBHW020305090426
42735CB00009B/1223